Life an alternative perspective

mad moose press

Managing Editors: Simon Melhuish and Emma Craven
Series Editor: Lee Linford
Contributors: Simon Melhuish, Emma Craven, Lee Linford, Nikole G. Bamford

Design: Alan Shiner
Illustrations: Justine Waldie
Photography: Getty Images

Designed and compiled by
Mad Moose Press
for
Lagoon Books
PO Box 311, KT2 5QW, UK
PO Box 990676, Boston, MA 02199, USA

ISBN: 1-904139-16-7

www.madmoosepress.com
www.lagoongames.com

Printed in China.

Life
Life Life
Life Life Life
Life Life Life Life Life Life
Life Life Life Life Life Life Life Life Life
Life Life Life Life Life Life Life Life Life Life Life Life Life
Life

Life can only be understood backwards, but it must be lived forwards.

Soren Kierkegaard

There is more to life than increasing its speed.

Mahatma Gandhi

Every one of us lives his life just once; if we are honest, to live once is enough.

Greta Garbo

Confused? Who isn't?

Just when you thought life was complicated
enough along comes a book that puts an
entirely new spin on its already countless
complexities and revelations.

Prepare yourself for an unconventional visual
journey through some of life's more significant
chapters, punctuated with a few words of
wisdom and some rather more conventional
interpretations.

fertilization ▶ *noun* (biology) the process by which an egg, female plant or animal is made fertile; the joining of male and female sexual cells to initiate development of life; application of fertilizer to soil, crops or plants to increase fertility (of land) or encourage growth.

fertilization

development

What grows makes no noise.

Proverb

development

birth ▶ *noun* the beginning of life.

birth

growth

**Intellectual growth should
commence at birth and
cease only at death.**

Albert Einstein

growth

schooling

Knowledge is power.

Proverb

schooling

change

**Adolescence is a period of rapid changes.
Between the ages of 12 and 17,
for example, a parent ages as much
as 20 years.**

Anonymous

change

destiny

One meets his destiny often in
the road he takes to avoid it.

Proverb

education

I have never let my schooling interfere with my education.

Mark Twain

education

graduation

religion ▶ *noun* worship, belief or faith in a supernatural power, typically a God or gods; an activity or interest pursued with obsessive enthusiasm or complete devotion.

religion

A man can know nothing of mankind without knowing something of himself.

Proverb

self-discovery

identity

Identity would seem to be the garment with which one covers the nakedness of the self, in which case, it is best that the garment be loose...

James Arthur Baldwin

0 41175 8007

identity

first job

first job

Success is often the result of taking a misstep in the right direction.

Al Bernstein

direction

twenty-something

If you want to be a
hundred you must
start young.

Proverb

twenty-something

career ladder

Careers, like rockets, don't always take off on schedule. The key is to keep working the engines.

Gary Sinise

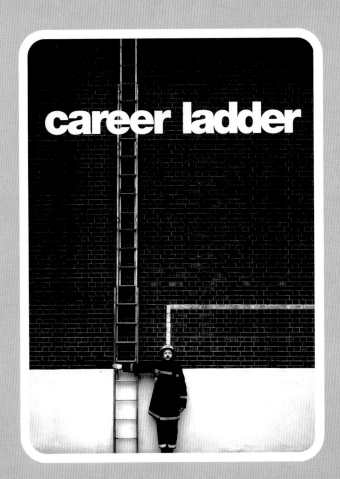

independence

independence

freedom ▶ *noun* liberty to act or speak without restraint or restriction; independence through self-determination; absence of commitment or responsibility.

freedom

social circle

Some cause happiness wherever they go; others, whenever they go.

Oscar Wilde

social circle

experimentation

If you don't make
mistakes you'll never
make anything.

Proverb

experimentation

relationship ▸ *noun* link, association or connection between people (esp. through marriage or bloodline), items or concepts; a state of interaction between people, establishments or institutions; an association of intimacy, emotional and sexual involvement existing between two people, usually over a period of time.

relationship

vision

Vision without action is a
daydream. Action without
vision is a nightmare.

Proverb

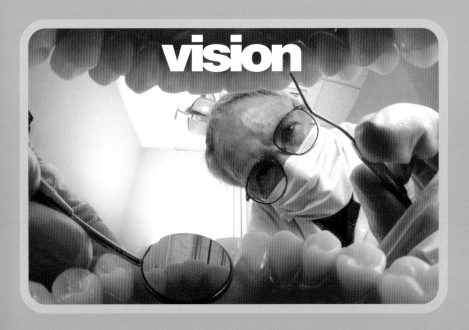

master plan

Everything has been figured out, except how to live.

Jean-Paul Sartre

Great oaks from little
acorns grow.

Proverb

prospects

responsibility

control ▶ *noun* the capacity to influence or determine the actions or movements of people or the outcome of a situation;

the power of restraint, self-restraint or self-regulation, particularly relating to an individual's emotions, actions or progress in a given situation;

an instrument or component of a machine, used to regulate its activity; central point from which systems, movements of people or plans of action are decided and implemented; a set procedure or benchmark by which the results of an experiment may be verified.

control

When written in Chinese,
the word crisis is
composed of two characters.
One represents danger and
the other represents opportunity.

John F. Kennedy

depression ▶ *noun* a feeling of despair, dejection or gloom usually experienced over a prolonged period; medical condition typified by exaggerated negative interpretation of one's circumstances, often accompanied by a lack of energy, concentration or interest in life; the action of applying pressure to push something down; a dip or hollow in the ground; a lowering of atmospheric pressure; the reduction of something, esp. economic activity, over a period of time.

self-improvement

self-improvement

strength

If only youth had the knowledge; if only age had the strength.

Proverb

maturity ▶ *noun* the state of having reached or achieved advanced or complete development, physically or mentally; coming of age.

maturity

marriage

integrity

What is wrong today won't be right tomorrow.

Proverb

integrity

relative ▶ *adjective* considered as being comparable, dependent upon or in proportion to something else; implying comparison to something else; linked or associated; (grammar) referring to an expressed or implied antecedent.

noun (of a person) belonging to or part of the same family, connected by birth or marriage

relative

routine

routine

breakdown

**One of the symptoms of
an approaching nervous
breakdown is the belief
that one's work is terribly
important.**

Bertrand Russell

breakdown

security

Moderate riches will carry you, if you have more you must carry them.

Proverb

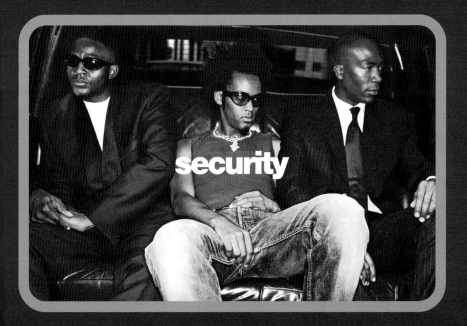

retirement ▶ *noun* the act of leaving employment or ceasing to work, usually upon reaching a specified age (retirement age); the period following the act of retirement.

retirement

ageing

A man as he manages himself, may die old at thirty or young at eighty.

Proverb

ageing

wisdom

**Knowledge speaks,
but wisdom listens.**

Jimi Hendrix

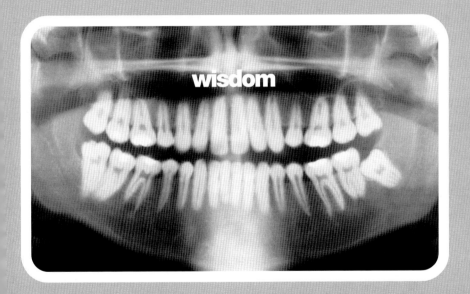

generation

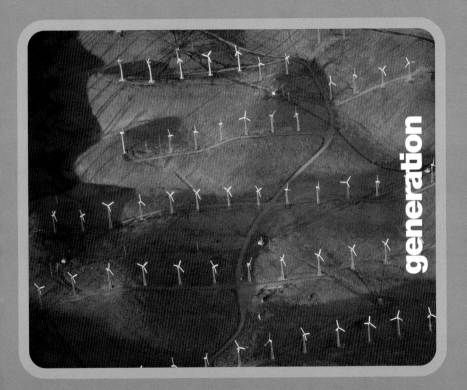

generation

death

After the game, the
king and the pawn go
into the same box.

Proverb

fulfillment ▶ *noun* (UK: fulfilment)

state of gratification or contentment resulting from the achievement of one's full potential or the refining of one's personal abilities or character; the completion of a duty or task as promised or required by condition.

fulfillment

Look out for the other titles in the Thought Provokers range:

Thought Provokers - LOVE
Thought Provokers - SPORT

mad
moose
press